Acknowledgment Unit photography by Alex Bailey

All Ladybird books are available at most bookshops,
supermarkets and newsagents, or can be ordered direct from:

Ladybird Postal Sales
PO Box 133 Paignton TQ3 2YP England
Telephone: (+44) 01803 554761
Fax: (+44) 01803 663394

A catalogue record for this book is available
from the British Library

Published by Ladybird Books Ltd
A subsidiary of the Penguin Group
A Pearson Company

LADYBIRD and the device of a Ladybird are trademarks of
Ladybird Books Ltd Loughborough Leicestershire UK

The Borrowers

Ladybird

The Lenders were just an ordinary sort of family with nothing unusual about them, though Victoria Lender thought her young son Pete had some weird ideas. He was always setting traps. Like now. She'd caught her finger <u>again</u>.

"I think that's enough traps," she told Pete as he freed her.

"Mum, just think of all the things that keep disappearing – Christmas tree lights, paper clips, candles, batteries…" he said.

"Something is stealing our things," he went on. "And I'm gonna catch 'em!"

Joe Lender came downstairs at that moment. "Shall we go?" he said to his wife.

"Where are you two off to?" asked Pete.

"To see Mr Ocious P. Potter, Great Aunt Mary's lawyer, about our inheriting this house," said Joe. "Fingers crossed, everyone."

They drove away in the car, and Pete left on his bike for school. Behind them the house lay silent.

At the lawyer's, Victoria and Joe had a real shock. "No will?" they said, looking at Mr Potter.

"That's right. Which means I have complete power to sell her house," said the lawyer.

"But we love that house, and she wanted us to have it. Can't we buy it?" asked Joe.

"I'm afraid not. I'm having it pulled down to make way for twenty-four luxury apartments. You have till Saturday to move out."

In the meantime, the Lenders' kitchen was quiet and still. Then it came alive once more as a tiny figure climbed onto the worktop. The little man, Pod Clock, rubbed his back and said, "I'm getting too old for this."

He was soon joined by his twelve year old daughter Arrietty, and his son Peagreen, who was ten.

"Borrowing time," said Arrietty. "Yippee!"

"Now," said Pod, "it's your first time borrowing, and there are rules. The main one is you must never, <u>ever</u> be seen."

Pod went off to borrow a battery, telling the children they must stay put. As usual, Arrietty paid no attention and started to climb the freezer. Soon she was trapped inside, getting colder and colder.

Pod heard Peagreen call for help, and raced to the rescue. But just as he got there, the front door slammed. The humans were back! Pod sent Peagreen home with the battery, then quickly showed Arrietty how to escape through the ice dispenser.

In the borrowers' tiny home under the floor below the clock, Pod's wife Homily was worried. "Oh my, where are they?" she said to Peagreen – just as Pod and Arrietty burst in. "There you are!" she said thankfully.

"Well, I couldn't leave Arrietty stuck in the freezer, could I?" said Pod.

"The freezer! Arrietty, you could have been squished, or frozen. Oh Pod, they're too young to start borrowing."

"They've got to learn," said Pod.

They had to stop talking for a moment or two as Victoria vacuumed just above their home. Then Pod went on, "Although perhaps you're right, Homily. Maybe we should leave it until the boy stops setting his traps…"

"Oh Dad! I'm not scared of that boy's silly traps," said Arrietty.

Her parents were shocked. "Beans are nothing but trouble for borrowers, and young beans are worst of all. Borrowers should never be seen or heard, it's very dangerous. But don't worry, love. We'll let you borrow again one day."

Later that evening, Homily went along to her daughter's room with a biscuit. She wanted to talk to Arrietty and make sure she realised just how dangerous beans and borrowing could be.

Arrietty didn't care. She really wished she could meet a bean!

Arrietty was about to get her wish. She was in Pete's room hiding among his toy soldiers when he suddenly looked straight at her. She was the most amazing sight he had ever seen. A real live girl, smaller than his little finger!

When Pete caught her and dropped her in the goldfish bowl, Arrietty put her hands on her head and said, "Go on, go ahead, bean."

"With what?" asked Pete, mystified.

"Squishing me, of course. We all know that beans don't like little creatures. Look at all those traps you've been setting."

"I'm not going to squish you," said Pete. "And what's a bean?"

"It's what you are – a human bean."

"You mean a <u>being</u>," said Pete, smiling. "I'm sorry about the traps. Anyway, our family's moving. You too, I guess. Mum says the house is to be demolished."

"Demolished? Why?" asked Arrietty.

"My great aunt left it to us, but she didn't leave a will. So now it belongs to Mr Potter, who's going to demolish it."

"This is a disaster," said Arrietty. "What's my family going to do?"

As it turned out, both families ended up moving together. Pete carried the borrowers in an ice cream carton. Pod and Homily were nervous—even more so when they lost Arrietty and Peagreen. The two fell out of the removal van as it drove off, but luckily

they weren't hurt. They walked back into the house wondering how to get to their new home. Then all of a sudden, Arrietty found an old map.

It was while they were working out which way to go that they heard the front door open. It was Ocious P. Potter – and he was looking for the safe where Great Aunt Mary had kept her will! He found it by tapping the wall with a hammer. Then he opened it by listening to the combination lock with his stethoscope.

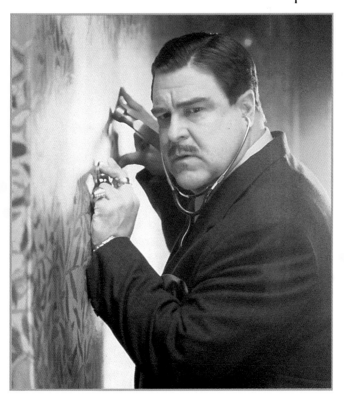

Arrietty and Peagreen were watching Potter through a vent in the wall. When the lawyer took the will from the safe, Arrietty realised what was happening. As Potter looked around for matches to burn the will, Peagreen and Arrietty crept out, grabbed it, and dragged it quietly back to their home. Potter turned round just as the will disappeared through the vent.

"If we can get the will to Pete," Arrietty explained to Peagreen, "we can save the house."

Listening through his stethoscope, Potter heard every word. He began looking for them, poking his fingers down the cracks in the floor. Arrietty jabbed him with their toasting fork. Then the lawyer forced up the floorboards, and was amazed to see the borrowers' tiny home.

There was no sign of the borrowers or the will, but he could see small footprints in the dust. Losing no time at all, he phoned his nephew, Exterminator Jeff.

Moments later, Jeff's van was outside the door. Potter took his nephew in to show him the tiny house. "Borrowers!" he exclaimed. "Little people! I've heard the stories, but never seen them."

"Never mind that, just get rid of them," said the lawyer.

Jeff pulled a mask over his face, then began to fill the wall near the borrowers' home with thick white foam.

Inside the wall, Arrietty and Peagreen were frantically climbing to escape the terrible foam. When they clambered through an opening onto the landing, Exterminator Jeff and the lawyer spotted them. They ran for their lives, but Potter was close behind. At last they managed to get away by sliding down the telephone wires from the roof.

Potter was still recovering from the chase when the doorbell rang. It was the local policeman, Officer Steady. Someone had been complaining about the banging 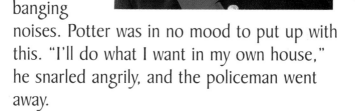 noises. Potter was in no mood to put up with this. "I'll do what I want in my own house," he snarled angrily, and the policeman went away.

Potter turned to his nephew. "How do we  find those little pests now? They've stolen something very important."

Jeff whistled, and a large bloodhound called Mr Smelly came padding up.

The two borrowers were in trouble again, because the bloodhound soon sniffed them out. Then Peagreen fell into an empty milk bottle and couldn't climb out. Potter and Jeff were just too late to catch him before the milkman collected the bottle. Mr Smelly followed the milk float, with Potter and his nephew close behind.

Pete had come back with Pod and Homily to get their children, and they saw what had happened. They too followed the milk float.

Behind them, Arrietty was crying her eyes out. Suddenly a voice said, "What are you crying for?" She whirled round to see another borrower – but one quite different from any she'd ever seen before. "I'm Spiller," he said. "What's wrong?"

"I've lost my brother. He fell into a milk bottle, and he's only little."

"Come on," said Spiller. "I know where he's gone, and I can get you there fast." He led Arrietty down to his rocket ship.

They climbed in and the rocket ship took off – down a long pipe into the Double Dutch Dairy. They saw Peagreen straightaway. Still in his bottle, he was heading towards the bottle washer. The bottle was washed and filled with milk before they could rescue him. Peagreen floated to the top, stunned.

But luckily Pod and Homily were at hand to help. As Peagreen went by them, they sailed into action. Pod knocked the bottle to the floor, where it smashed to pieces. There was a worrying moment before Peagreen opened his eyes. Then he said fiercely, "I <u>hate</u> milk!"

Moments later, Arrietty and Spiller came through the milk hatch to join the others, and they all smiled happily. Suddenly a large shadow loomed. It was Potter – and <u>he</u> wasn't at all happy. Arrietty and Spiller had managed to cover him with tons of cottage cheese. "My, what a treat!" he said furiously. "The whole thieving family together! Here, I'll take that…" And he snatched the will from Arrietty's backpack.

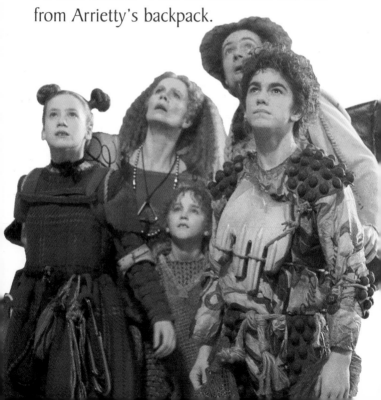

Potter hadn't finished with the borrowers. He stuck them down one by one under the cheese chute with sticky tape, then pressed the cheese fill button firmly, and left for City Hall. He had a demolition to register! As Potter drove off, Pete found the borrowers and set them free. Arrietty's first words were, "Pete, we've still got time to save the house!" To Pete's surprise, Exterminator Jeff, who was fed up with his uncle's greed, took him to City Hall in his van. Pete went straight to the Town Planning Office.

The borrowers went to City Hall in Spiller's rocket ship, and got there first. They managed to lock Potter in a store cupboard, then tied him up.

The cupboard was suddenly full of borrowers, and Homily and Pod found many old friends — even some relations.

But when footsteps were heard, a thousand borrower heads whipped round. Every borrower disappeared — and, as if by magic, Potter was no longer tied up. In came Pete with Officer Steady. Pete took the will from Potter's pocket. "See, I told you he had it. This proves he was trying to cheat us out of our house."

Officer Steady read the will and nodded his head. Slowly, he pulled out a pair of handcuffs. It was jail for Potter!

Next day the Lenders were back in their old house. They invited Officer Steady and Exterminator Jeff (not forgetting Mr Smelly) to a party. "We just want to say a big thanks for saving our house," said Victoria.

Down below, the Borrowers were happy to be home once more. They were having a party as well, with friends they hadn't seen for years.

But Spiller and Arrietty soon disappeared – to the rocket ship. Fast was fun – for both of them!